31 DAYS TO AN UNSTUCK AND INSPIRED YOU

Uche Unogu

Onyx Evangelistic Ministry

Indianapolis, IN USA

http://evangelistuche.com

uche@evangelistuche.com

+1 (317) 409-9829

ACKNOWLEDGEMENTS

I want to thank Pastor John Lubhaya of New Jerusalem Charitable Society for allowing God to use him to inspire me to complete this book. I am grateful for my audience, who read and commented on the content here. Your votes were used to select the content that made it to this book. But mostly, your vote of confidence, your questions and requests for prayers inspired the content. I am thankful for the stability provided by my family. Last and not the least, I am thankful to God, who chose me and continues to use me. Indeed, I can do nothing on my own, but with Him, there is nothing I can't do.

TABLE OF CONTENTS

DAY 1 - BE DESPERATE FOR THE GIVER, NOT THE GIFTS

received correspondence from a lady whom I will call Betty. Betty sounded desperate to get married within the year. She gave her increasing age as a reason to settle down now whatever it takes. She is dating a man who requested intimacy before marriage which she, being a Christian, turned down. The man has now moved another woman into his apartment who has no problems yielding to his sexual requests. Betty feels like she has to give in to the man's demand so that he would chase the other woman away and marry her. She is also contemplating allowing the man to date two women as long as he marries her. Bottom line, marriage is not eluding her this year. What desperation.

Rebecca was a virtuous woman who, though wanting to be married, never went around in hot and desperate pursuit of a man. I am certain she was prepared to live life fully, with or without a man. Rebecca was beautiful and very well brought up. The Bible said, she had known no man. She just went about her daily duties, adhering to the godly ways her parents raised her. She saw a stranger one day who appeared tired from a long trip, and displayed her hospitality by heeding his request for water. She not only provided water for him alone, but also for his cattle. She didn't know this stranger was on a mission to find a wife for the son of the great Abraham. How could she have known that the same cattle she was nourishing would take her to her husband's house? How could she have known that one act of goodness would lead to her becoming the mother of Jacob, from whom the nation of Israel emerged? How could she have known?

Ladies, the man should pursue you, not the other way round. Just go about your business doing the Lord's will. He sees you. He knows your needs. He takes care of His own. Trust in His wisdom and judgment. Trust that He has your best interest at heart. If that means going a lifetime without being married, that's hard, but so be it. Don't be desperate for a husband, be desperate for God. Men, don't be desperate about a promotion or a job, or even a wife. Go about seeking His Kingdom and its righteousness.

Don't be desperate for the gift, be desperate for the giver.

For when you attain, the giver, you attain His gifts. When you are desperate for Jesus Christ, he gives you that which is only yours, and no devil under torment can snatch it from you.

His gifts are without repentance but they have to be His gifts, not something you gifted yourself with.

Don't allow external pressures like your age, status, or people's opinions, drive you to desperation. Instead, allow your internal craving for God lead to His good and perfect will.

And in that day seven women shall take hold of one man, saying, we will eat our own bread, and wear our own apparel: only let us be called by thy name, to take away our reproach. Isaiah 4:1

DAY 2 - CHRISTIANITY IS NOT ABOUT RULES, IT'S ABOUT LOVE

I am horrible with cramming/memorizing. I can if I have to, but I'd rather not. I would rather understand a topic or issue well enough to discuss it in my own words. My mind should be able to "wrap around" the topic, then "devour and digest" the topic into my spirit. This enables me to share the topic with conviction and passion, rather than just standing as a stone, speaking merely out of memory recollections. You may be this way as well. With this backdrop, imagine then, how I felt about Christianity when someone introduced it to me as a book of rules. How could I memorize all these rules of do's and don'ts and then strive to obey them daily, flawlessly. These rules here mentioned are a major dissuading factor to many wanting to follow the straight and narrow way.

Imagine again the relief I felt, the joy unspeakable that flowed through the sinews of my being, when I learned that Christianity was not about rules, but about love. A love relationship with the king. A love affair between

Jesus Christ and myself. Yes, there are the rules, but all these rules are enraptured in the commandment "...Thou shalt love thy neighbor as thyself" Romans 13:9. In a relationship, you love the other person insomuch that you do not want to hurt them. You do your best to be there for them when they need you most. You are faithful because your love for the other person surpasses that of any other person. There is trust you can't betray. Christianity is likewise, not about rules, but about LOVE.

Perfect love casts away all fear, including the fear of death and hell. It's not about, "if I break one rule, God will cast me to hell ". It's about:

I love God so much I don't want to hurt Him today.

He has done so much for me. He has taken away my sorrow oh glory hallelujah, He is coming to take me home. And for that, the least I can do is love Him more every day. I am not perfect, I make silly mistakes. Mistakes that are too embarrassing, but this I do, I reckon myself to be dead to sin and alive to righteousness. I strive to love Him more perfectly each day. There is no denying my love for Him. He is my sufficiency. He is my all in all. He is the object of my worship. He is the love of my life.

This is Christianity. Christianity is not about rules, it's about LOVE.

Love worketh no ill to his neighbor: therefore love is the fulfilling of the law. - Romans 13:10

DAY 3 - TRUST, TRUST, TRUST IN THE LORD!

I was recently invited to ride in the car of a university administrator, and I obliged.

Michael it was who had asked me to leave the country, as a student, if I could not afford my fees. That was many years ago. We had since become fast friends. He asked favors of me as the local neighborhood coordinator, and I was mostly willing to accommodate him. As we rode, he told me how he struggled to trust God. He believed that God gave Him a brain and that He should use his brain to figure things out (this is true). The problem was that he became anxious and worried when he could not figure things out. He relied so much on his brain to bail him out of situations. Sound familiar?

It was Job who made the immortal statement, "Though He slay me, yet will I trust Him ". In the days of plenty, Job trusted God. In the days of scarcity, Job still trusted God. In sickness and in health, Job's trust was unwavering. When his friends, and even his own wife asked him to curse God and die; Job was steadfast in his trust for God. God restored to Job all He lost, with interest. You see:

Trusting God is not a luxury. It is a necessity.

It is needed to wade through life victoriously. Needed to keep your head when others are losing theirs. I could go on and on, but you get the point.

Back to Michael, I told him that we are called to trust and obey. Have you ever felt like you can do anything because someone else trusted that you could? I believe God feels the same when you trust Him, and is well pleased. God commands you, His child, to trust him just like you trusted your parents as a child. Trust that He has your best interest at heart. Trust that when things get really nasty, He will sustain you. Trust that He wills a desirable end for you. Trust that He has got the situation under control. Trust that He will never leave nor forsake you. Trust that the righteous is never forsaken nor do his children beg bread. Trust, trust, trust in the Lord.

Beloved, I wish above all things that thou mayest prosper and be in health, even as thy soul prospereth. - 3 John1:2

DAY 4 - MAKE THE MOST OF YOUR SITUATION

The King of Syria laid siege to the city of Samaria causing a famine so great that the people resorted to cannibalism, as has never been seen before. They proceeded to kill and eat their own children that they may live another day. It was in this situation that four lepers made a decision that changed their lives forever. They reasoned that if they stayed where they were (outside the city gates), they would die, for there was no food there. If they went back into the city of Samaria, they would die as well, for the famine was great. But if they moved forward to the enemy's camp, perhaps the Syrians would have mercy on them, or kill them. Either way, that was a much better option.

When the lepers got to the Syrian camp, they found the camp deserted, with food and supplies laying waste – all for their taking. They ate to their satisfaction, saved for their retirement, and then called others to partake of the spoils. These lepers, instead of bargaining to eat themselves, made the most of their situation.

It's been cold here in Indianapolis. Really, really cold. But it's been good. As I traverse this beautiful city, in elevators and in parking garages, I hear people complain how they are "so over this weather". I see the depression written all over people's faces as they go through their daily routines. The winter has been long and the temperature has dipped lower than -5 degrees Fahrenheit, too many times. I am not oblivious to these realities. But it's good. Why is it good you may ask? Let me give you three practical reasons why it is good:

1. It is good because you get to stay indoors. When you are indoors, you spend more time with your family. You get to see your spouse and children more. This is sometimes not appreciated enough until someone has to leave the family for six months on a military deployment.

2. It is good because you get an opportunity to read. Since the warmest place available to you is your home, you might as well stay in and read. All those life changing books you have not read simply because you've been busy running from pillar to post. Well, now you can stay in and get that reading done.

3. It is good because you get to save money.
    Granted, the gas heating expenses will rise
    sharply, but you will notice that your
    penchant for shopping on impulse will reduce
    as well. Since its cold, you now have to plan
    the times you go to the store rather than
    stumbling in there by accident.

I share this to let you know that you can turn a
potentially negative situation into a positive one.
It's all in your mind, it's all in how you choose to
approach the situation and, how you respond to
it. Try to see a positive in every negative. Treat
every emergency leisurely. Remember that God
is not asleep, He watches, He is on the throne, He
is in control.

> **...Why sit we here until we die? If we say,
> we will enter into the city, then the famine
> is in the city, and we shall die there: and if
> we sit still here, we die also. Now
> therefore come, and let us fall unto the
> host of the Syrians: if they save us alive,
> we shall live; and if they kill us, we shall
> but die. 2 Kings 7:3-5**

DAY 5 - IN THE FULLNESS OF TIME

I was once in a hurry, desperate even, to travel to Europe and ply my trade as a professional soccer player. I trained hard on the pitch, and made the necessary moves to obtain a visa. Unfortunately, things were not working out as I had hoped. To put it in Basketball terms, "Shots were not falling ". It took me a while to realize that God was not going to allow me go anywhere until I was ready. In the meantime, I had to learn to study my present environment and ask God, "Why did you put me here? What are the advantages of being in this position? What are you trying to teach me by keeping me here?" God began to speak to my spirit that I had to bloom were I was planted. That I had to be present.

Some things, like entrepreneurship, are not necessarily learned in the classrooms but on the street and, on the job. And so I became present, and started to make the most of my situation. As I started to prosper in my environment, in the fullness of time, an opportunity opened to go to the US to study. I almost revolted, but I had learned enough not to question God from arrogance, but to humbly ask: "Lord what would you have me do?" That is how I got to where I am today. As an evangelist, I continue to ask: "Lord, what are you doing now?"

There is the story of the 10 virgins, 5 wise and 5 foolish. What made the wise virgins wise, was simply the fact that they brought reserves of oil with them, they had savings. Whereas the foolish ones did not have reserves and so had to go buy some more oil when theirs were exhausted. In the fullness of time, the Bridegroom arrived and only the 5 wise virgins were there to meet him. The 5 foolish virgins couldn't go into the wedding ceremony because they were not present when the bridegroom arrived.

Appreciate where you are at the moment and be present. There is a reason God has put you were you are. Study your environment and understand its strengths and weaknesses. Also understand that there is a time for everything.

God's timing is best. He is never a minute early, nor a minute late. He always shows up in the fullness of time.

Are you in a waiting phase now or trying to figure out your next move in life, yet "shots are not falling?" "Chill", it will come together in

God's timing. Don't make any desperate moves, don't give up on God, and don't settle for less. Wait on the Lord, and be present, for in the fullness of time, He will show up big time. He always does.

But when the fullness of the time was come, God sent forth his Son, made of a woman, made under the law ...- Galatians 4:4

DAY 6 - BE THANKFUL FOR YOUR HATERS

Many years ago, as a recent high school graduate, I had people in my house block tell me that I would not amount to much. That they would be the world changers, and I would be lucky to just get a roof over my head. I cringe now to think that I believed this. I went online and applied to several Universities in the United States and around the world. And guess what? Almost all of them replied to me. Imagine then, how my "haters" felt when they saw top Universities send me mail wooing me to apply. The funny thing is that the mail came through them because they were the mail receptors for the block. They became the carriers of good news to me. They delivered my blessing to me.

Haman hated Mordecai simply because Mordecai did not bow to him. As such, Haman hatched a plan that would lead to the destruction of Jews. In this plan, Mordecai was to be hung on a gallow. Earlier, Mordecai had unraveled a plot to murder the King but was not rewarded for his efforts. One day, the King decided to reward the man who had saved his life, and asked Haman what should be done. Haman, thinking he was the one to be honored, suggested that the honoree be treated as royalty. And so the King commanded Haman to treat Mordecai as royalty across the kingdom. Think of that: God blessed Mordecai, not behind Haman's back, but in his full presence. In fact Haman, the hater, was the one to deliver the blessing to Haman in the full awareness of everyone.

Don't feel strange when God blesses you. Don't try to explain it or apologize for it. Just look pretty and give all thanks to God. Give Him His due for He is worthy of your praise.

Use the accompanying platform to tell the world how good a God you serve.

God seldom blesses you behind the backs of your haters. He does it in their presence.

In fact, he makes them deliver the blessing to you. Be thankful for your haters today!

Thou preparest a table before me in the presence of mine enemies: – Psalm 23:5

DAY 7 - GET BACK UP AGAIN!

Christie (not her real name), a former college colleague, was suffering from low self-esteem and had made some recent poor decisions. There was a feeling that this was the way it was always going to be. That she had blown it and would continue to make bad decisions moving forward. That she had sinned away her day of grace. Things were in turmoil at the moment and she didn't know what to do. She had deviated from the Christian way since graduating from college but wasn't sure she wanted to go back to the Church. I encouraged her not to give up but to keep trying. Who knows if all this present turmoil wasn't a wakeup call from God so she could return to her first love? A prodding to get back up again.

David committed adultery, fathered a child outside wedlock, and worse still, murdered a man. The child he fathered became sick and struggled for life. David refused food or drink as he interceded for the child's life. In spite of David's repentance and intercession, the child died. Remarkably, as soon as the child died, David got up from his slump, ate, drank, and went about dispatching his duties as King. This was not the only time David had to bounce back from failure. Once, his son took the Kingdom from him. The men around him were discouraged but the Bible says David encouraged Himself in the Lord. He got back up again and conquered. Perhaps that was one of the things that made him a man after God's own heart. The fact that he always got back up again.

You may have failed last night, but today is a new day. God's mercies are new every morning. Great is His faithfulness. Don't stay down. Don't give up. Get back up again. Dust yourself up and keeping pushing. A saint is just a sinner who fell down, BUT got back up. It's not how many times you fall that counts; it's if you get back up. You've got unlimited grace, so why limit yourself to the ground? Get up! You've come this far, in your Christian walk, why disbelieve now? Only believe. The devil is a liar. The fact you failed does not mean you are a failure. You are victorious because you get back up again. God is counting on you. Get back up again!

It is of the LORD'S mercies that we are not consumed, because his compassions fail not. They are new every morning: great is thy faithfulness. - Lamentations 3:22-23

DAY 8 - YOU HAVE ATTAINED, NOW HELP OTHERS ATTAIN

As an 18 year old young adult, just starting out in ministry years ago, I remember telling a friend that all I am to achieve, I have already achieved. In other words, there is nothing bigger or greater for me to attain. It sounded proud and foolish at best, but allow me to explain. You see, as a young man, I was fortunate enough to know Jesus Christ, and have Him as my Lord and Savior. Many have to wait till they are much older, sometimes on their death bed, before they acknowledge Christ. Yet I know that my knowledge of Christ comes with a solemn responsibility. An important question is asked of me daily, "What are you going to do with this Jesus called Christ?"

Pontius Pilate once had the savior at his mercy. He could release Him or sentence Him to death. It was his choice and he knew that to release Jesus was the moral thing to do. His wife cautioned Him to do the right thing and send the innocent man home. Pilate, asked the immortal question that is asked of us Christians (rephrasing): **"What shall I do then with Jesus Called Christ?"**

Instead of answering his question, he differed to the mob. He allowed this precious treasure to be killed and buried.

What are you going to do with this Jesus called Christ? Will you keep Him buried in yourself or will you release Him to the world? Will you keep your mouth shut as to how the Lord has been good to you, and watch many die not knowing or experiencing the same goodness? You have attained Christ, the ultimate prize. Congratulations. Does it now mean you should coast through life? No, God forbid. To whom much is given, much is expected.

You are to spend the rest of your life communicating this prize to others and, opening the door of opportunity to others, not slamming it shut behind you. You are to share this Jesus Christ, this good news, to others who need to hear it. Now that you have attained, help others attain.

> **Pilate saith unto them, What shall I do then with Jesus which is called Christ? ...**
> **Matthew 27:22**

DAY 9 - GOD'S TIMING IS THE BEST

In early 2013, I completed the recording of a song "Praising Your Name". It sounded good and I wanted as many people as possible to hear it. God put in my heart, the concept of a radio campaign. I approached a local radio station about premiering this song and a few others on air. The radio station was all ears but didn't seem to follow through on the opportunity. I had felt strongly that it was God asking me to premier the songs on radio, and so I was disappointed, but I soon got over it.

A year later, I was approached by a radio station who found me on twitter - notice I did not approach them. They wanted to interview me and premier my songs. When I heard this, I just laid on my bed speechless. I asked, "Lord what are you doing? How gracious you are".

God promised David the throne, but he did not attain to it within the year. God promised Abraham a son, but he did not attain it within the decade. God promised to remove His children Israel from slavery but it did not happen overnight. God's promises are true regardless of the timing. He didn't say when He would do it, He just said He would do it. That should settle it.

Delay is not denial. When you are down to nothing, God is up to something. The desire God placed in your heart may have not been accomplished this year, but it doesn't mean it won't be done. If God's hand is on it, then it will surely happen.

Trust God with all your heart. He will bring your deliverance speedily. He is not slack to accomplish all that concerns you today. His word will never return to Him void. Has He said it, He will do it in your life. Believe that God's timing is the best.

God is not a man, that he should lie; neither the son of man, that he should repent: hath he said, and shall he not do it? or hath he spoken , and shall he not make it good? - Numbers 23:19

DAY 10 - IT'S BETWEEN YOU AND GOD

My mom, a fire brand Christian and born again to the core, took me with her as she went about planting Churches. In my early youth, I followed her to countless night vigil sessions of praise and prayer. I found myself in Church every single day of the week. I heard way too many sermons and at some point suffered from sermon burnout. I stepped forward to give my life to Christ way too many times. I felt pretty confident that based on my mom's effort, and based on my hanging out with church folks all the time, my way to heaven was paved and guaranteed. But this assumption was wrong. God showed me that He is the guarantee to heaven and that I must come to Him myself. Nobody could or would do it for me. Not even my mom. And so I developed a personal relationship with God that changed everything.

The sons of a high priest once took it upon themselves to challenge devils based on the Jesus that Paul preached. Their dad was clergy and they had perhaps, seen Paul preach and cast out devils a few times, so they felt very qualified to do the same based on their proximity to religion. They said: "We adjure you by Jesus whom Paul preacheth". Notice that it was not the Jesus that they preached, but the Jesus that Paul preached. Needless to say, the devils replied: "Jesus I know, and Paul I know; but who are ye?" They were pounced upon and subdued.

You can't inherit Jesus. You have to accept Him. God is not your grandfather, in-law or uncle. He can only be your Father. You can't merit His power based on the works of your parents. You have to stand alone with and in Him. It's got to be your personal relationship with God that saves the day. Your pastor can add his faith to yours, your pastor can intercede on your behalf and expound the gospel to you better. But at the end of the day, it's between you and God.

Jesus saith unto him, if I will that he tarry till I come, what is that to thee? Follow thou me. - John 21:22

DAY 11 - LET IT COME TO YOU

When I started my career years ago, I competed to be the administrator for a Nurse Triage Software Application. The competition was bitter and left me at odds with my co-worker. As the battle raged, I was offered a dilapidated system with no users nor prospect for success. Nobody wanted to be its administrator, so they gave it to me, and I accepted. Six years later, this dilapidated system gave me renown throughout the organization of 16,000 employees. More than 3,000 of them used it regularly. My promotion was swift and that bode well for my ability to provide better for my family. Guess what happened to the software application I fought for? Well, the Nurse Triage group was dissolved in a massive layoff and its influence subsided. This is just one of so many examples in my life, where I have been taught that the things I didn't struggle for were the things that stayed the longest. The things that came to me, had the most lasting influence, utility and satisfaction. Let it come to you.

Perhaps, you've heard of the apostle Peter trying to show solidarity to his Lord. How that he picked up a weapon and slashed off the ear of an assailant, only to verbally deny his Lord within a few hours. He hustled, and tried to do it in his own might and failed. But when the Holy Spirit fell on Him, out of windows and doors, and into cities he went, proclaiming the good news about his Lord. He began to show solidarity almost effortlessly. You know of Moses trying to free the Israelites with his bare hands, and how miserably he failed. When He met God in the burning bush, the story changed. He became a one-man invasion, going into Egypt to defy the mighty Pharaoh, with the words: "Pharoah, let my people go ". Do you get the point? Let it come to you.

Are you fighting for something that should be fighting for you?

Are you fighting people as though your fight is against flesh and blood - just so you can get? Are you burning bridges that ought to be repaired and fortified? You forget to be kind to people, to show Christ love - just because you want it, oh...you want it so bad, you forget what really matters - people. Nishan Panwar puts it this way: "Sometimes it's not about the journey or the destination. But about the people you meet along the way".

In life, you will find that the things that are mostly yours are the things that come to you.

Of course there is work to do. You have to be receptive, and realize when these things come and embrace them wholeheartedly. But stop fighting everybody just so you can get ahead. Let it come to you.

DAY 12 - WHAT THEN ARE YOU AFRAID OF?

Once, I was given 2 months to find a new job. This does not seem too bad when you are single and somewhat free, but with a family to provide for, this is terrible news - or is it? Could it be that God was up to something again? Could it be that God was saying, "You've been on this mountain too long, it's time to move ahead?" Oh, it was hard to choose which voice to believe. Do I believe the voice that said I was doomed, and all hope was lost? Or do I believe God's promise that this was only the beginning of greater things?

Noah was ridiculed for building a boat, when there was no evidence that it would rain. The naysayers were scientifically backed by the fact that rain had never destroyed the earth till that point. Noah's only proof was that God said it and He believed it. After building the boat and placing his family in it, God shut the door, but the rain did not start immediately. It was days before the first drop of rain fell. Oh, I imagine how hard they laughed at Noah, saying: "Where is the rain you so certainly spoke about?" But you see, God promised it, and He would do it. Noah believed this and that was the difference between life and death for him and his family.

Do you believe God's promises? God has provided everything that pertains to you in this life to live righteously. It will not be provided, **it is already provided.** God has given you eternal life, so there is no earthly doom to be afraid of. God has promised that ALL things are working together for your good so long as you love God and are called to His purpose. God said that you should be anxious for nothing, but rather lift up your concerns to him in prayer - with thanksgiving.

> **God has said He will never leave nor forsake you. He said when you pass through the valley, He will be right there walking with you. What then are you afraid of?**

DAY 13 - GOD'S LOVE IS THE ONE THING CONSISTENT

My life has been full of ups and downs. There have been moments when I felt on top of the world, and moments when I felt I didn't belong. Over time, I've learned to take these feelings in stride. Many times, they are just what they are - feelings, and nothing more. Other times, they are pointing to an issue I must work through. I've found the one thing I know that is consistent, God's love. He loves me in the good times and in the bad times. God's unyielding love for me makes it all worthwhile.

David had high and low times. One time, he killed Goliath and the entire nation of Israel erupted in admiration, chanting his name. Another time, his own son took the throne from him and sought to kill him. He disgracing him by sleeping with all his concubines publicly. What shame that must have been, but David took it in stride. Through his failures and his successes, in His highs and in his lows, he knew God loved Him and had called him to His purpose.

This same God will come through for you. In the low times, consider. Consider how good the Lord has been to you. How He has brought you to the place you are now. Consider how He has lifted you each time you fell down. How He caught you each time you fell. Consider then how that He has gone to prepare a place for you. That where He is, you may be also. Has He done it before, He will do it again. The future is bright. This too shall pass. You've prayed, so it's not in your hands now. It's now in God's hands. Don't do anything drastic or stupid even. Just watch Him come through. God's love is the one thing consistent.

In the day of prosperity be joyful, but in the day of adversity consider ... - Ecclesiastes 7:14

DAY 14 - HOW TO HANDLE AGGRESSIVE CO-WORKERS

Throughout my professional career, I've had the privilege of working with some excellent and talented people. However, there are always that person that seems to make things a little harder than they should. I will use the term "Aggressive Co-worker" to describe this person. I am not the only one who encounters these folks, everyone seem to have these. Perhaps you do too. I've learned they will not go away, (unless you want to live in your basement the rest of your life). The key issue is learning to work with them and still keep your joy, your peace and above all, your righteousness. It is doable.

Jesus had his own aggressive co-workers to deal with. They were supposed to be co-laborers in building the Kingdom of God. They were the Pharisees and the Sadducees. elders and leaders in the church who didn't like the "competition" Jesus brought. Occasionally, Jesus took them on, other times, he marveled at their ignorance, but mostly, He did not allow them stop the work He came to do. Jesus always had the big picture before Him and stuck to His work irrespective of the jealousy and murder threat he faced. In doing so, He, Jesus, left a wonderful example for us to follow. Don't forget the big picture. Don't forget why you came here in the first place. Take it all in stride, including the insults. Finish and get what it is you came here for.

These aggressive co-workers want what you have and are willing to fight you for it.

Ignore when you ought to, confront when you must, but mostly, keep your laser focus and smile.

Don't allow anyone break your focus. As much as is in your power, opt out of the situations that brings you and the aggressor together. Let them have the project or whatever it is they are trying to win from you. If it was meant for you, it will come back to you because their skill and capabilities will not be able to get it done. Most importantly, humble yourself, pray for the aggressive co-worker, and just keep moving forward.

Woe unto you, scribes and Pharisees, hypocrites! for ye are like unto whited sepulchers, which indeed appear beautiful

outward, but are within full of dead men's bones, and of all uncleanness. - Matthew 23:27

DAY 15 - IF GOD GAVE IT TO YOU, IT'S YOURS! DON'T WORRY

There have been a few situations where I was challenged over a position God gave me. A position in which I did not struggle for nor did I get of my own might. Yet through sheer will, someone tried to usurp it. I did try to fight back for my rightful position in the past, but over the years, as I matured as a Christian, I learned to let go and let God. God admonishes many times in the Bible to remain meek, to not return evil for evil, and to be patient with all men. In these situations, God fought for me and restored my position. Many times, I have had to pray for those who tried, of their will to usurp my God given authority.

Miriam and Aaron once spoke against God's servant Moses. They accosted him, asking if God only spoke to him. They alluded that God also spoke to them, too. In other words, they challenged the authority God gave to Moses. They were in fact saying, "You are not the only leader here, we are leaders too with the same authority that you have". Moses did not have to do or say anything. He just remained meek. God

Himself came to His defense. God called Miriam, Aaron, and Moses out and clarified that Moses had the mantle. As for Miriam and Aaron, God's anger was kindled against them and Miriam was struck with leprosy. Moses, in his meekness, prayed for her deliverance and she was delivered.

When people try to usurp the authority God gives you, allow them. Don't be rude to them or try to fight them. Don't argue or bear a grudge. Allow them. If the authority wasn't theirs to begin with, it will crush them. With this understanding, do you now see why it's important to pray for those who try to dislodge you or who scheme to take that which God gave to you? God is watching, He will restore it to you. Nothing to worry about. His gifts are without repentance. If God Gave It To You, It's Yours! Don't Worry.

And Moses besought the LORD his God, and said , LORD, why doth thy wrath wax hot against thy people, which thou hast brought forth out of the land of Egypt with great power, and with a mighty hand? - Exodus 32:11

DAY 16 - 5 THINGS DAD TAUGHT ME ABOUT SUCCESS

I do not recall ever being very close to my dad. I would see him perhaps once or twice a week, and then only for brief moments. I fondly remember him coming to the house occasionally and taking my elder brother and me for car rides. We would, on purpose, take routes riddled with speed bumps just so we can yell "Pogom" as we went over one. Good times. When I was in-between high school and college, my dad took me under his wings. This season lasted about 13 months and I learned a lot about what it takes to be successful. There are more, but I will briefly touch on a 5 of these:

1. **Humility:** My dad was a multimillionaire at his prime, yet you would never know it by looking at him or by observing the lifestyle he lived. He was the everyday normal guy. He dressed normal, rented apartments, drove normal cars, and sent his children to normal schools - nothing too flashy. I learned firsthand that he who would be lifted up must humble himself. Humility opens doors and grants deep insight into mankind in general.

When you understand men, it would not be too difficult to garner from them that which you need to be successful.

2. **Hard Work:** Dad plunged himself deeply into his lifework. He met deadlines consistently, produced high quality content, and showed up daily. He always topped his peers at what he did. Dad told me, "If you can do anything to near perfection, the world will beat a path to your door ". I never did forget this wise saying.

3. **Do what you love:** Dad did what he loved - Chemistry. In high school and college, dad noticed that Chemistry came easy to him. He struggled in other academic concerns but not Chemistry. He didn't have to study hard like the other students did for Chemistry, it just came to him. And so when it was time for him to choose a career path, he picked the Chemistry field. No wonder he excelled at his work. He loved it and was passionate about it. I learned through Him to stay within the field of my gifting. I don't mind doing other things, so long as they are helping me get to where I can do what I truly love. To succeed, you need to put in the hours. This becomes easier if you are doing something you love.

4. **Think:** It was Rene Descartes that remarked: "I think, therefore I am ". One of the things that separates us from animals is our ability to think. Dad is a deep thinker. He would sit alone, sometimes in the darkness, and ponder the issues on his plate, and make decisions accordingly. He thinks about what was said yesterday, and about where he wants to be 5 years from now. He outsmarts his competition over and over again. He outthinks his friends and "out-strategizes" his opposition. His insight into issues are remarkable and from Him I learned to "**give it some thought** ". Thinking can be tedious and is sometimes hard and painful but must be deliberately undertaken to succeed.

5. **God:** I didn't get my Christianity from my dad. I got that would from my mom, but I did gain a deep appreciation for spirituality through him. Man is a spiritual being. Dad dabbled in spirituality. He understood that his power over his peers is spiritual and he found solutions to problems spiritually. He once commented that: "God would have struck me dead if not for the wife I married. When He tries to punish me for my wrongs, He looks to my dear wife and refrains because of her. He does not want to hurt her". Dad did not know this, but his

statements here are scriptural. The non-believing wife or husband can be covered by virtue of his/her spouse.

There you have it. These are 5 things dad taught me about success. But here is the real success: God found me at a young age and has been the most instrumental in teaching me about success. Mostly, God helps me define success. Success to me is not in the big house, fleet of cars, and/or access to the finer things of life.

Success to me is living each and every day as a son of God

What my dad taught me helped me navigate the issues of life that pertained to dollars, but what God taught me about success helps me navigate life itself.

But first the kingdom of God, and his righteousness; and all these things shall be added unto you. - Matthew 6:33

DAY 17 - GOD'S GOOD PLEASURE

I pray for people daily. The testimonies pour in but for some, the answer takes a little longer to show up. Whether you've gotten your miracle or are yet to get it, what binds us together is our thanksgiving and unyielding faith. God is faithful. Has He said it, He will do it. His ways are not your own and His timing is not exactly yours but in the fullness of time, He will come through for you. He never fails. Heaven and Earth will pass away but His word will remain. Anchor your trust deeply in His word.

Some of the things you pray for are in line with your will - nothing wrong with that. And some of the things you pray for are God's will. If you pray for God's will, you can start rejoicing after you ask because it is His good pleasure to give it to you. It is God's good pleasure that you are provided for and are content. It is His pleasure that you abstain from fornication, and that you live a holy life. It is His good pleasure that you give thanks to Him in all circumstances. It is His good pleasure that you lead a quiet and peaceable life in all honesty and godliness. It is God's pleasure to reveal Himself to you that you come into the knowledge of truth.

It is God's good pleasure to save you. Have you been abused in the past? Your innocence wrongly taken from you? Your heart ripped out and stomped upon right before your eyes? Have you been through the loss of a job or the loss of a provider (parent or spouse)? You who were well taken care of all of a sudden find yourself on the street corner begging for assistance? Let me say unequivocally that God's sees you. He knows you. It is His good pleasure to give you wisdom. It is His good pleasure to show Himself strong on your behalf. To avenge you the wrongdoing you suffered. It is your Father's good pleasure to give you what you ask of Him. It is His good pleasure to rescue you from the depths of hell. So don't worry little Child. It is your father's good pleasure to give you the Kingdom.

Fear not, little flock; for it is your Father's good pleasure to give you the kingdom. - Luke 12:32

DAY 18 - STOP AND TAKE STOCK

Every now and then, I STOP and take stock of where it is I am and where it is that I am going. Sometimes, I am able to travel to faraway cities and from the outside, look in. Other times, I am unable to travel but I try not to miss an opportunity to STOP and take stock. The reason for this is simple. It is easy to continue on the bush track without realizing that the bush track is taking you to a place you don't want to go.

It is easy to be engrossed in the day to day and forget where it is you are going and what exactly it is you are trying to accomplish. Before you know it, 5 years have gone by and you have not yet achieved anything of significance. Yes, you've paid the bills but what other than that? A co-worker once told me, "Uche, I have not accomplished anything this week, but I am certain I have been busy ". Sound familiar?

The Israelites wandered the desert for 40 years. They were moving quite alright but they were not going anywhere. There was activity but no accomplishment. There was busyness but nothing to show for it. God, through Moses, told them that they had been in that situation too long, and it was time to make progress. **It was time to stop majoring on a minor.** It was time to stop chasing shadows but instead pursue the real thing. It was time to STOP, take stock, switch direction, and make progress.

You have a unique opportunity to make a difference, to be a life giving spirit. To mold generations to come. Don't waste it in vain pursuit of materialism. Don't blow it in a persistent effort to get even. Don't drown your life away in bitterness and un-forgiveness - in striving to prove a point, in craving to be respected. Try to see the big picture. Don't get indefinitely caught up in the day to day operations. Once in a while, look up and ascertain if you are on the right track. Do a rough calculation to see if the miles ahead of you are less than it was the last time you checked. Be thankful for the past. Live in the present, hope and plan for the future. Stop often and take stock.

The LORD our God spake unto us in Horeb, saying, Ye have dwelt long enough in this mount: - Deuteronomy 1:6

DAY 19 - LET IT GO

Riding back from a family visit, the passenger; I will call Lola (not real name), mentioned how something was said to her and it really hurt her. It had been over 6 weeks since the statement was made but she said thinking of the statement made her cringe with pain. I informed Lola that many people get Cancer just by holding on to some hurt caused by someone else. Bitterness of any kind does not just hurt the bearer emotionally, but eats you physically as well in terms of health. The solution, not easy I know, is to let it go.

Not for the other person who planted the seed of hurt in your life, but for yourself. Forgiveness does not mean you have to trust the person again. It just means you have let the offense go - let it go. You are perhaps well versed with the story of the prodigal son. A boy loved deeply by his father chose to employ betrayal by asking for his inheritance prematurely and choosing to leave his home for a faraway land. When children begin to ask for inheritance, it sometimes hurts the parent because it is assumed the child wants the parent dead so they can get an inheritance. As hurt as the dad was, he did give his son the inheritance and bade him farewell. He cried day and night watching as the days turned to weeks, and the weeks to months, and the months to years.

One day as the dad sat on his roof, He saw his son coming back. In that moment, he forgave all that the son did wrong, ran to him, and embraced him back. The father did not die of grief partly because he let it go.

What is that thing you are holding within you that should be let go? What is that offense someone, perhaps a spouse, did that you are yet to forgive. What is that bitterness eating you inside? It needs to go. Don't allow that person rule you, let the peace of the Holy Spirit flood your soul instead. There are 7 billion people in this world. Don't let that one person cause havoc to the glorious future God has in store for you. Let it go today.

For if ye forgive men their trespasses, your heavenly Father will forgive you: - Matthew 6:14

DAY 20 - WHERE YOU WANT TO BE

Basketball athlete, LeBron James, wrote a letter to Sports Illustrated explaining his move from the Miami Heat back to his hometown team, the Cleveland Cavaliers. The sentence in the letter that stood out most to me is: "I learned from a franchise that had been where I wanted to go ". Think of that for a minute. LeBron went to Miami because it had achieved what he was trying to achieve. In other words, Miami had felt what he was trying to feel and for him to feel that, he had to go to a place that had known that feeling. And he did know that feeling - he won two championships.

I think of Christianity in the same light. If you are reading this, it means you have never been dead, so let me ask, what does it feel like to be dead? You won't have a clue because again, you have never been dead. You have never lived a year, perhaps a week without sin - what would it feel like to go a lifetime without sin? What does heaven look like? A sure way to answer this is to go to someone who has been there, done that, and align yourself with that person. Jesus Christ is that person. **Run To Jesus.**

Do you want to live abundantly and righteously? Do you want to have great relationships or a great career? Scripture tells us that Jesus Christ has been where you want to go. He has tasted celebrity, victory, fame, renown, and success. He has tasted failure, betrayal, depression, anxiety, fear, and death. Run to Jesus Christ today. He can help you get to where you need to get to because He has been where you want to be.

For in that He Himself hath suffered being tempted, He is able to succour them that are tempted. Hebrews 2:18

DAY 21 - DIFFERENCE BETWEEN AN AMATEUR AND A PROFESSIONAL CHRISTIAN

Growing up, I had dreams to be a professional soccer player. That did not materialize as God called me to a different path - to ministry. I still remember the joyful feeling I had when I first saw my name listed as a Systems Professional. I had just secured employment with a Hospital system as a Business Analyst and was thus considered a professional. What then is the difference between an amateur and a professional?

An amateur pays to do a task, while a professional is paid to do the same task.

People are willing to wait in long queues, travel for miles on end, and offer their hard earned money to benefit from the work of a professional. How then do you graduate from being an amateur to being a professional? The answer is in putting in the time required and the practice necessary to attain near perfection in your craft. Like my dad told me:

If you can do anything to near perfection, the world will beat a path to your door.

How does this all link to Christianity? Paul in his letter to the Hebrews wrote about two kinds of Christians; the amateur and the professional. He admonished that when the people ought to be teachers of the law (professionals), they still needed to be taught (amateurs). He said they were still drinking milk (amateur), when they ought to be eating meat (professional). This validates that there are varying levels of Christianity. At the base, the milk Christian is still saved and will go to heaven because they believe in the Lord Jesus Christ, just as the meat Christian would, but Paul was calling the Hebrews to a higher level of Christianity. In essence, he was calling on them to graduate from Amateur to Professional Christianity.

How then do you become a professional Christian?

You become one by constantly and persistently exercising yourself towards Christianity. Thereby developing the fruits of the Spirit.

These fruits, according to Galatians 25:22-23 are: love, joy, peace, longsuffering, gentleness, goodness, faith, meekness, and temperance. There may be a couple of spiritual gifts sprinkled into the mix as well.

An amateur Christian is like the biblical seed without deep roots. The presence of stormy weather can cause this Christian to stumble, falling back head first into sin. An amateur Christian is also someone who still drinks the milk part of the word and has not yet embraced/graduated to eating the meaty part. For example, this person believes, and rightly so, that Jesus Christ died for her sins but struggles to believe that He who is of God does not sin because they cannot sin.

At its core the difference between an amateur and a professional Christian is the presence of Spiritual fruits.

For when for the time ye ought to be teachers, ye have need that one teach you again which be the first principles of the

oracles of God; and are become such as
have need of milk, and not of strong meat.
Hebrews 5:12

DAY 22 - WITH GOD'S CALL COMES HIS PROVISION

An invitation to preach at a Crusade in India was delivered to me one day. It felt right. I prayed about it and got the confirmation to accept the invitation. Filing out the visa application was a hassle so I decided against it but I did notice they had an embassy in Chicago. My brother in-law came to visit us in Indianapolis, and asked if I could drive Him up to Chicago to catch his flight back home. I recalled my Indian invitation and so agreed thinking I would be able to visit the embassy and drop Him at the airport. I was thoroughly blown away at how God provided everything we needed within walking distance. I needed a Walgreens store to print my passport photo and there was one right there. I needed a FedEx store to perform my printouts and again, there was one nearby. When I got to the embassy, there was only one person ahead of me in line. Within a few minutes, I had an Indian visa. God is in the little things.

God spoke to Jeremiah, informing Him that He had placed a call on His life, and that it was time for him to speak. Jeremiah was not to be afraid of people's faces but to speak boldly the words God put in His mouth. God said He would provide the words, the audience, and the opportunity to speak - all Jeremiah had to do was to speak boldly. There was a promise that though people will fight him, God will personally deliver and protect Jeremiah. And there also was a consequence that if Jeremiah did not speak, he would be confounded right in front of his hearers.

God's call comes with a promise and a consequence.

Has God called you to ministry, yield to this call. I tell the testimony above to let you know that with God's call, comes His provision. Has He called you to it, He will make a way for it. Trust that He who called, is faithful to take care of His business. This is inspiration to all those that have felt the tug of God's call in their heart. To those that want to do ministry but feel the opportunities are not there or that they are not well prepared.

God does not call the qualified, He qualifies the called. And with God's call comes His provision

But the LORD said unto me, Say not, I am a child: for thou shalt go to all that I shall send thee, and whatsoever I command thee thou shalt speak. Be not afraid of their faces: for I am with thee to deliver thee, saith the LORD - Jeremiah 1:7-8

DAY 23 - GOD IS YOUR PORTION

Growing up, God impressed upon my young heart to serve Him as an Evangelist. He brought me in close proximity with role models that I admired greatly. I was either in the Church, or attending evangelistic meetings. I saw firsthand, the sick get healed, the unemployed get jobs, and the destitute find Christ. As I grew older, I noticed occasionally, that the fine admiration God put in my young heart for His servants, sometimes manifested itself in jealousy. I began to wonder why his dad was a great preacher who laid a platform for his ministry, while my dad was not.

God showed me in these times that He and He alone establishes His ministers. That He, not the crowd nor accolades, is my sufficiency. In other words, having Jesus Christ is enough. He is all I will ever need.

The King of Sodom admonished Abraham to keep the goods he obtained from battle and give up the people he got. Abraham replied that he didn't care about the goods, and it should not be known that anybody but God made him rich. In other words, He didn't care about becoming accomplished from worldly sources. His source of wealth came from God. He did instead pay his tithes to Melchizedek, the King of Salem. God spoke to Abraham shortly after this act, informing him:

I am thy shield, and thy exceeding great reward

Our gifts vary, not by mistake, but by divine purpose. We are all different for a reason. That we complement each other, and become one in Christ. There is a fine line between admiration and jealousy. A line between being accomplished by worldly things and being accomplished by having Jesus Christ. God is your portion. He is your satisfaction. He is your sufficiency. He is your all in all. It's easy to fall into the trap of jealousy. That the other person has this and you don't. That they get to go here or do this, and you don't. When these dark thoughts cloud your mind, shine a ray of enlightened light through it - **that God is your portion and your ever present helper.**

After these things the word of the LORD came unto Abram in a vision, saying, Fear

not, Abram: I am thy shield, and thy
exceeding great reward - Genesis 15:1

DAY 24 - GOD SAID IT, THAT SETTLES IT

God called me at an early age but I ran away from this call, wanting to be soccer star, an Information Technology guru, anything but one preaching the gospel. I mentioned this earlier in this book. I gave excuses: how can a boy from Nigeria, West Africa preach around the world? But God said it. My travel application was rejected twice but God said it. I didn't have the money to pay my school fees, but God said it. I graduated with a Master's Degree. Today I preach the gospel around the world. Why? God said it, and that settles it.

God warned Noah about an impending disaster. A "flood-pocalypse", if you will. Noah was commanded to build an Ark, warn people to repent of their ways and invite them to join him in the ark. By faith Noah built this Ark even when there was no history of rain water destroying the earth. He was mocked and proven to be wrong scientifically, yet he soldiered on. Embedded in his action was a deep faith that God said it, and that settles it. **A faith so strong, a trust so**

secure, a hope so solemn bore Noah in executing His life work. The Ark was built, and Noah went in with his family but it did not rain immediately. I imagine the mocking he got. "Didn't you say it will rain?" Noah was steadfast, God locked the Ark, and rained the earth into oblivion. God said it, and that settles it.

Through my Story, Noah's story and many more stories, I pray you are encouraged to develop a quiet trust in God, an unshakeable Faith. A hopeful confidence that God will always come through. That He takes care of His own. Has He said it? He will do it. God said it, and that settles it. His word is His bond. His call is firm and His gifting permanent. Faith Trust and Hope encompassed in one. God will not let you down. He has your best interest at heart. It is not by your power nor by your might but by God's Spirit. It's not your will power or your relentless energy, but it is of God showing you mercy.

For he that is entered into his rest, he also hath ceased from his own works, as God did from his. - Hebrews 4:10

DAY 25 - GOD FIGHTS FOR HIS OWN

As a young University Soccer player, I experienced the wrath of a new coach whom didn't want me in his team from day one. He came in with his own players and complained about the others he inherited. He refused to honor my soccer scholarship commitment, leaving me, as an 18 year old to bear the full brunt of my school fees. In that moment, I felt the world was over. I felt I was being crushed. Five years later, I looked back and noticed God paid my fees and made something out of me. As for the soccer coach, I wonder where he is today, but I pray God's hand of forgiveness is upon him. This season of life taught me that God fights for me even when I can't see His hand.

The Children of Moab and Amon once came to fight the Israelites. Israel's King Jehoshaphat fasted with the Israelites and prayed a solemn prayer reminding God that He brought them to where they were today and that He owned the land. God told the Israelites not to worry because it was His battle. There wouldn't be a need to do anything other than sit, praise, and see the power of God. The Moabites and the Amonites turned against each other and were vanquished. The Israelites took of them, riches so great that they could not contain it.

In life, many will rise and fight you for no just reason. Instead of panicking and worrying, see the situation as an opportunity for God to display His power. See it as an opportunity to gain spoils. See it as a launching pad to the destiny God wants to bring you. In the past God fought for you. What makes you think he won't fight for you now? Many have been your adversary yet God has always sustained you. He is not about to stop now. God put you in the position you are in. He is very able to sustain you. God's hand is upon you. He is able to steer you out of temptation. He is able to get glory from your situation. Always remember that God fights for His own.

Thus saith the LORD unto you, be not afraid nor dismayed by reason of this great multitude; for the battle is not yours, but God's. - 2 Chronicles 20:15

DAY 26 - WHAT IS GOD DOING NOW?

It was the beginning of October. We had spent most of the year paying down huge financial obligations; such as the house, and were excited the year was almost over. All was well until my company announced that there was going to be some job eliminations. I felt bad for those that were about to lose their jobs and didn't give it a second thought since I was excellent at what I did - or so I thought. I was on my computer one day and received a meeting invite from the departmental head. I felt a knot in my stomach. The same knot I felt when I was refused a visa many years ago. The same knot I felt when I lost everything on an international trip.

I walked into the boss's elegant office and there was told that my job had been eliminated. I had 2 children at home, a wife, and numerous financial obligations - and here I was jobless. I was downcast, depressed, frustrated, scared - you name it. It took me a few days to muster enough courage to tell my wife what had happened. She in turn told me she was pregnant.

Think of that. We were expecting a new baby, and I had just been laid off. How would we pay the medical bills? How were we even sure we will not be out sleeping on the streets soon? Oh, this was the worst season of our lives, or was it?

No. As soon as I heard she was pregnant, my depression left. I felt joy. I knew God will never give us this child if He wasn't going to provide. I finally asked that immortal question: What is God doing now? And God answered deep in my spirit. I could see now that He was enlarging our coast. That he was helping me quit a job I was so scared of quitting but should have. He was telling me that an era was coming to an end, while a new one was dawning. I smiled lovingly at my wife as the revelation hit. We named the child "Akuchi", meaning "God's wealth".

Within a few weeks, I was offered new employment that was less stressful and paid way more. I got the job title that I had dreamed of having for years. My old company provided a generous severance package which enabled us to expand and take the long trip we had always wanted. I say this testimony to inspire someone today. Maybe that's you. Are you going through really hard times? Could it be that God is trying to make a decision for you that you are too scared to make yourself? Could He be moving you from one era to another? Have you asked, "What is God doing now?"

Believe it or not, God is working. Through the shame, the tears, and the heart ache, He is doing something new.

You are being downsized so you can be uplifted. You are taking a step backwards so you can lunge 3 steps forward.

Now it is on you to ask and find out, what God is doing now?

But without faith it is impossible to please him: for he that cometh to God must believe that he is, and that he is a rewarder of them that diligently seek him - Hebrew 11:6

DAY 27 - LOYALTY

There is the story of a man who died one day and went to heaven. He was being judged before the pearly gates, and was asked, "When you were on earth, did you ever steal, lie, and cheat?" In the midst of a bright light, he could but tell the truth. He remembered the ills he had done and confessed to them. Then it was told to him that only perfect people could enter heaven and that he should turn to leave. Just then, Jesus Christ stepped into the scene and said, "This man, while he was on earth did steal, lie, and cheat. He was a sinner but this one thing he did do. He stood for me. Now I am going to stand for him and take his place."

The moral of this story is that God rewards loyalty. Loyalty will take you far. Loyalty will take you past the bumps and temporary setbacks of life. Loyalty will help keep you safe. In the long run, loyalty is rewarded.

King Ahasuerus could not sleep one night. He asked his servants to bring the records books and read to him. In it, He found out that a Jew named Modecai had once thwarted a plot by 2

assassins to murder him. The King also noted that
nothing was done to reward Modecai's loyalty
to him. The King then commanded that Modecai
be brought and rewarded accordingly. Modecai
was promoted for his loyalty. Later a man
named Haman hatched a plot to get rid of
Modecai and the Jews, Modecai asked the
Queen Esther to make a request of the King for
his life, and that of the Jews. She did, and
Modecai was saved and again promoted for his
loyalty.

**If your wife is loyal, then you have a gem in
your hands, of priceless worth.** A man with a
wife who is not loyal can hardly go anywhere
far in life any more than Samson could with
Delilah.

> **Enemies from the outside cannot touch
> you. Those that can touch you are
> disguised as friends, those embedded deep
> within your inner circle.**

Betrayal is one of the most painful and
devastating acts in life. You may not be
perfected yet, but strive to be loyal to God and
His cause. He sees past the outward appearance
and the outward service. He sees the heart and

intentions. He never fails to reward those that are loyal to Him and those that speak on His behalf and take sides with Him. Many times, good things we do out of loyalty seem to be forgotten, but I want to assure you that loyalty is never forgotten forever. It is always rewarded.

Whosoever therefore shall confess me before men, him will I confess also before my Father which is in heaven - Matthew 10:32

DAY 28 - SOMETIMES YOU WIN, SOMETIMES YOU LEARN

I once was involved in coaching 6-7 year old children in soccer. Our first two games were a disaster. The problem was that we did not dedicate players to man the defense. But we learned from this failure. We adjusted, we grew in confidence, we learned to utilize each player's capabilities, and we learned how to lock up our defense. By the 3rd game, we had started winning. We didn't lose another game till the end of the season. Parents walked up to me and said thank you. They had seen their children go from losing games to winning - all because we learned from our mistakes.

Moses tried to rescue his fellow brothers, the Israelites, with his own might. He failed. 40 years later, he tried again and this time, he succeeded. What was the difference? Moses learned from his failure. He learned that it was not by might nor by power, but by the leading of God's Spirit - Zechariah 4:6. He learned it was not he that willeth nor he that runneth, but God who shows mercy - Romans 9:16. Moses learned not to lean on his own understanding, but to trust in the Lord with all His heart - Proverbs 5:6. Moses' loss was devastating at the time and led to his exile. But he learned from it, tried again, and succeeding in fulfilling his calling - getting the children of Israel out of Egyptian bondage.

Failure is the tuition paid for success.

Loses are devastating. Nobody likes to lose. I don't have to tell you 100 reasons why losing sucks. I will, instead, tell you one reason why it is good. That reason is that you get to learn. Sometimes you win, sometimes you learn. It's difficult to learn from success because of the popular dictum, "Why fix it when it is not broken".

When you win, and I pray you do often, you only seek to repeat what worked for you. You don't as a matter of fact, delve into what wrong was masked by the success. When you lose, you stop and take stock. What did I do wrong? How can I improve? You learn, you make adjustments, and you win. Sometimes, this takes more than one iteration but the end result is winning.

Though he were a Son, yet learned he obedience by the things which he suffered - Hebrews 5:8

DAY 29 - HOW TO HANDLE STRESSFUL SITUATIONS

A woman was caught in the act of adultery. It was a dire situation. She was to be stoned to death, and now. The Scribes and Pharisees came to Jesus Christ to ask what He thought about the issue. It was urgent, an emergency. The woman was about to die and perhaps the opinion of Jesus would save her or damn her. Hurry Jesus, hurry, give your opinion. If I were thrust in this situation, I wouldn't be surprised to see myself panting and eager to come up with a quick fix, but what did Jesus do? He stooped down and began to draw with his fingers as though He did not hear them. In other words, He approached the stressful situation with calm and composure. He treated the emergency leisurely. He collected His thoughts, He communed in Spirit with His Father, and then he gave a response that saved the woman's life.

Many times in my career, I've had to deal with stressful situations. Many times, I allowed the "Lizard brain" to kick in. Oh, I'm not going to make it OK; oh, and my leader is going to be mad at me, oh, oh oh! When I lose my composure like this, I most likely end up on the losing end. But when I apply the techniques below, I come out higher than I went in. When faced with a stressful situation, an emergency if you will, strive not to lose your composure. Calm down and evaluate, don't make decisions hastily. Really, really, really, calm down.

Below are 9 tips I've garnered along the way to help you deal with stressful situations.

A challenge is just an opportunity for you to move up the ladder, for you to be promoted - if you come out victorious.

1. Continue to be nice and agreeable as much as is in your power to all that come across your path.
2. Don't allow the stress get to you.
3. Continue to be positive.
4. Listen to a sermon and/or listen to some encouraging Christian music.
5. Read the scriptures and meditate on it.
6. Step away from the situation and take a walk.

7. Reminisce on how good God is and how He has brought you this far.
8. Concentrate your thoughts on the positive and not the negative.
9. Say "Ouch". When someone is extremely mean to you via email or in person. I learned this technique from a former boss and it helps disarm the person causing stress, buying you time to make a seasoned move.

Stressful situations are what they are, stressful. But you don't have to be stressed or have a nervous meltdown just because there is stress around you. God gives you His own peace for troubled times. He gives you His peace to keep you, and to help you keep your head while others are losing theirs. That they may, through you, know that He is.

Peace I leave with you, my peace I give unto you: not as the world giveth, give I unto you. Let not your heart be troubled, neither let it be afraid. - John 14:27

DAY 30 - DESPISE NOT WHERE YOU ARE

When I first came to the United States, I only had a traveling bag that I dragged down National Avenue en route to the University of Indianapolis. Hidden in my socks was money to last me through my first semester. I was just a young 18 year old filled with dreams and excited about the possibilities in front of me. Little did I know that I was in for a rough and bumpy ride. The smooth sailing myth that hovered over my head like clouds over the earth, imprinted by Hollywood movies, soon bust. Reality set in. In retrospect, I am grateful I did not despise my little beginning. It all happened so lives could be saved.

David started out as a Shepard of a few sheep. Perhaps his herd grew as he gained competence. He had a knack for playing the harp but there was no audience for his hobby. So you know what he did? He played for the sheep he was herding. David was faithful in the little that he was given. He didn't despise his day of small beginnings. He played, content with the card he was dealt in life. Little did he know that one day, he would play his harp before the King. Little did he know that one day his renown would sweep Israel. His name would be chanted in harmony with the King's name - and even in greater light:

Saul has killed his thousands and David has killed His ten thousands.

You see, David eventually became King and better yet, he became a man after God's own heart. Do not despise your humble beginnings. **Don't be comfortable with it nor settle in nicely, but do not despise it.** Take inventory of where you are now because you will never be here again. Learn all you can in the phase of life you currently are in because lessons learned will help sustain your rise.

Be content but not complacent. Thank God for now, but also ask Him for your tomorrow. Live in the present, but be mindful of the future.

Your present is molding your future. Your humble beginning is forging in you; the fortitude to take the future hits and triumph. Greater things are ahead because you despise not where you are today.

**For who hath despised the day of small
things? ... Zechariah 4:10**

DAY 31 - THOUGHTS ON LOVE

I was approached, on more than one occasion, by a fashion magazine to write something on Love. I brushed the request off but as the request kept coming persistently, I thought it expedient to think about love and pen something very brief and accurate about it. The most important thing that comes to my mind about love is not the love I have for my wife (though that is very important). It is the love God has for mankind. The God love. Agape. The love that prompted God to GIVE His only son. He loved so much that He GAVE. This kind of love is not deserved, neither is it earned. It is unconditional.

When you love, you give. How do you know when you love? It is when you give of your time, treasure, and affection to someone else.

Love is not a feeling, it is a decision.

In order words, Love is less about what you feel, than what you do. Love is a verb, an action word. Love is active. Love is about giving more than it is about receiving.

Love is letting down your ego boundary so that it can accommodate someone else. Love is being committed to the spiritual growth of someone else. Love is extending yourself to others. Love is correction. Love is so much more. Love is God and God is Love.

Love is not always reciprocated but it is never lost nor wasted. It comes back in one form or the other. Love is selfish and selfless at the same time. For in giving love to others, you show selflessness, yet the rewards of giving love unquestionably are immense hence the selfishness of Love. Love is staying when the going gets rough. Love is sticking it out with someone else. Again, love is God and God is Love.

He that loveth not knoweth not God; for God is love. – 1 John 4:8

31 DAYS TO AN UNSTUCK AND INSPIRED YOU

A 31 DAY DEVOTIONAL THAT WILL INSPIRE YOUR CHRISTIAN WALK AND HELP YOU MOVE FORWARD.

UCHE UNOGU

www.ingramcontent.com/pod-product-compliance
Lightning Source LLC
Chambersburg PA
CBHW021138020426
42331CB00005B/826